The Cornish Seashore

Endymion Beer and Trevor Beer

Tor Mark Press · Redruth

The Tor Mark series

Cornish titles
Ancient Cornwall
Birds of Cornwall
Charlestown
China clay, traditional methods
Classic Cornish anecdotes
Classic Cornish ghost stories
Classic folk tales from the Land's End
Classic ghost stories from the Land's End
Cornish fairies
Cornish folk-lore
Cornish inventors
Cornish legends
Cornish mining industry
Cornish mining – underground
Cornish recipes
Cornish saints
Cornish seashore
Cornish smuggling industry
Cornwall's engine houses
Cornwall's history – an introduction
Cornwall's railways
Customs and superstitions from Cornish folklore
Demons, ghosts and spectres from Cornish folklore
Do you know Cornwall?
Fed fitty
Introducing Cornwall

Lost ports of Cornwall
Pasty book
Shipwrecks around Land's End
Shipwrecks around the Lizard
Shipwrecks on Cornwall's North coast
Story of St Ives
Story of the Cornish language
Story of Truro Cathedral
Strange tales of the Cornish coast
Tales of the Cornish smugglers
Twelve walks on the Lizard
Wild flowers of the Cornish coast
Wild flowers of the Cornish hedgerows

Devonshire titles
Birds of Devon
Classic Devon ghost stories
Devon customs and superstitions
Devon legends
Devon seashore
Devonshire jokes and stories
Shipwrecks of North Devon
Wild flowers of the Devon coast
Wild flowers of the Devon hedgerows

West Country titles
Classic West Country ghost stories
Clotted cream
Pixy book

First published 2001 by Tor Mark Press, PO Box 4, Redruth, Cornwall TR16 5YX
ISBN 0-85025-387-X
© 2001 Endymion Beer and Trevor Beer
All rights reserved
Printed in Great Britain by R Booth (The Troutbeck Press), Mabe, Penryn, Cornwall

Introduction

The Cornish seashore is a friendly place loved by thousands of visitors and locals for recreation or holiday. It's a spot to watch the waves pounding, to relax in deckchairs or generally to wander, unwind and feel the fresh air and the sea spray.

And if you take the time to look more closely, there's another beach world to enjoy – patterns in the sand, seaweed curling round wooden posts, shells and rock pool life, footprints left by other creatures, and perhaps birds feeding among the shingle beneath the dunes.

This book explains what to keep an eye out for in this ever changing habitat and how to recognise a few of the commoner yet interesting animal and plant species. All it takes is common sense and a respect for nature that is as necessary here as elsewhere in the countryside. Remember the Country Code.

Sadly, these days another note of caution is also needed. With each successive tide, debris is brought onto the shore by wave action. The 'strandlines' may possibly contain dangerous items such as glass and tins which can cut the feet of the unwary, or oil that can be both messy and potentially dangerous. Wherever you are, if you observe pollution, the Environment Agency Emergency Hotline is Freephone 0800 807060.

Tides and wave patterns

Never forget for a moment that tides occur twice daily. Printed tide tables are available at bookshops whilst tide times are usually featured in local newspapers and on television daily. Every year there are avoidable accidents involving people being cut off by the tide or swept out to sea by unexpected currents.

Wrought by the power of wind and waves causing sand movement, beautiful patterns are displayed on sandy seashores where the sea has recently been. These patterns serve to remind us that the tide ebbs and flows twice every day. Once a fortnight 'spring' tides, which have a wide range between the high and low points, dictate the boundaries of the shoreline. In alternate fortnights 'neap' tides occur: these have the smallest range between high and low water marks.

Even the movement of this moored rowing boat as it is shifted by the tide clearly shows as lines in the seashore mud. Walking the seashore looking for such signs is good fun and can soon make you a nature detective with a much greater awareness of this marvellous environment.

A typical West Country cove, with rocky headlands to either side and a sandy beach exposed at low tide. Each part of the cove has its own specialised wildlife

Types of shore

The seashore is a harsh place subject to more extremes than any other natural environment. In Cornwall tides vary enormously and seashore types range from sheer cliffs to gently sloping sands or mudflats. At Hayle and Perranporth, for example, the beaches are formed from blown shell sand, calcium rich, a none too frequent occurrence in the South West.

At other beaches you may find interesting geological bedding planes or shingle, rocks and sea-worn pebbles. Each seashore is a turbulent, constantly changing world which supports diverse plant and animal life, the latter often visible from the thousands of shells left scattered about.

If you would like to find out more about the local geology, 'Holiday Geology Guides' can be obtained from British Geological Survey, 30 Pennsylvania Road, Exeter, EX4 6BX, or from Cornwall RIGS Group at 5 Acres, Allet, Truro TR4 9JD.

The 'splash zone'

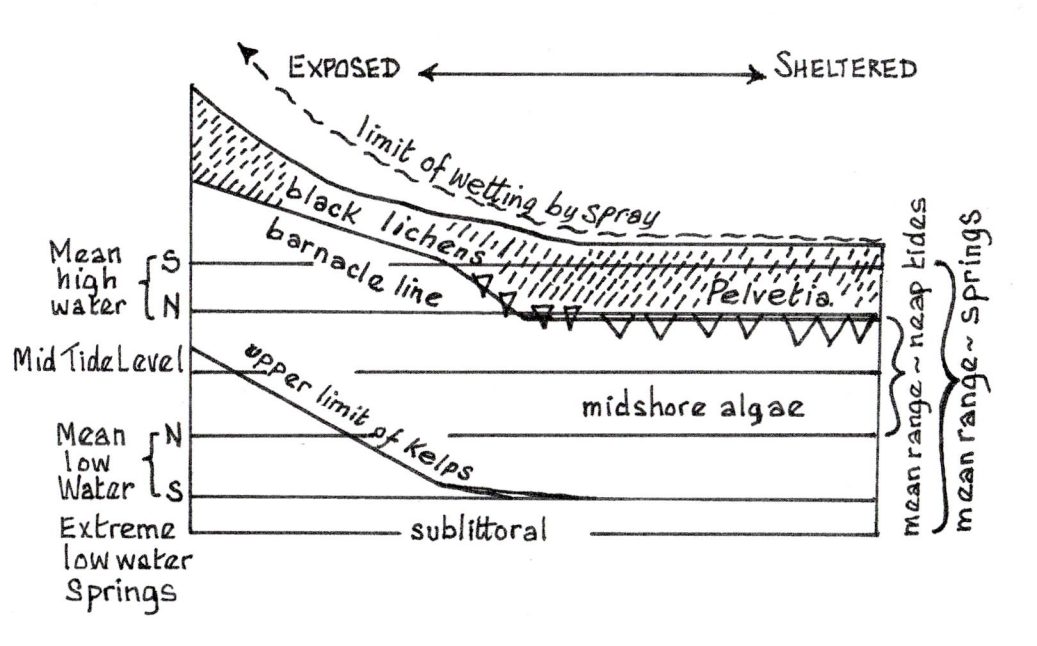

Tide terminology and some of the zones to be found on sheltered through to exposed shores. (N = neaps. S = springs.)

Sea defences: groynes

These timber frameworks, also called breakwaters, are to be found on several seashores. They are built to control sea encroachment by checking wave action: sand and shingle is swept from one side of the groyne and piled up on the other where it is moved onshore at right angles to the waves. Wooden groynes are useful sites to look for the wood boring gribble, a tiny isopod (marine crustacean) which lives and breeds in the tunnels it makes in the timber. There can be as many as several hundred gribbles to the cubic centimetre.

Sea defences: chestnut paling fences

These are often erected in dune systems where gales and storms regularly 'blow out' the existing sand. A common conservation and management method, they trap the windblown sand and thereby help to form new dunes.

The young dunes can then be stabilised by Marram grass which is a coarse perennial with sharply pointed greyish-green leaves and can grow up to 120 cm tall.

Above: Chestnut paling fences are used to stabilise the blowing sand

Below: Marram grass spreads quickly in the dunes and binds the sand

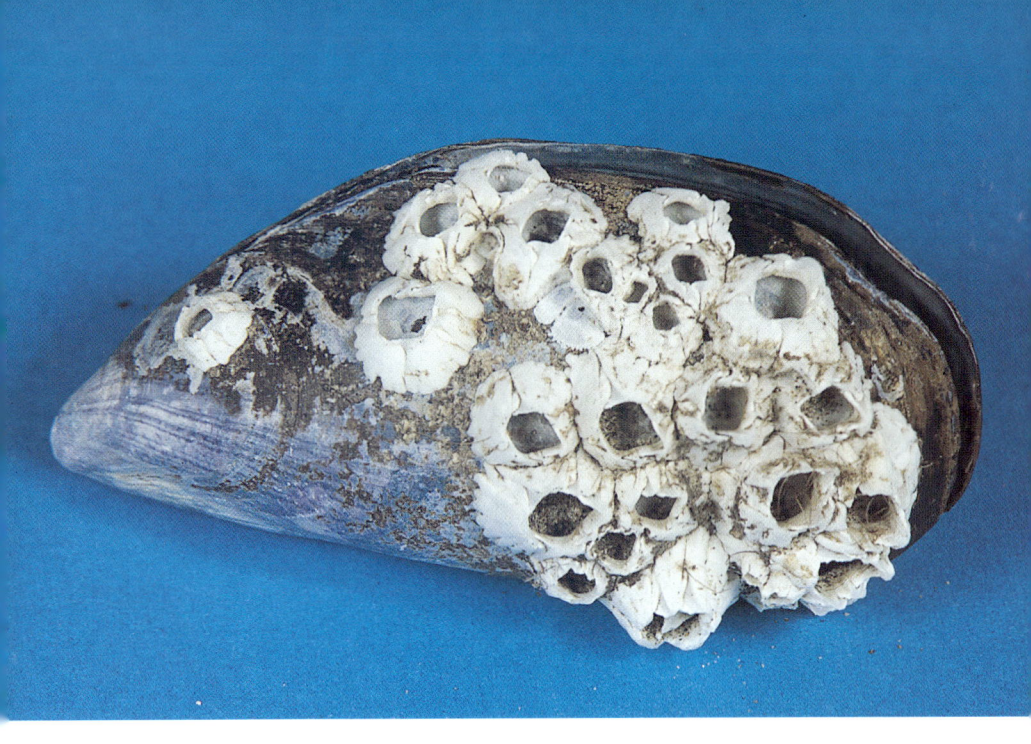

Common mussel, covered with barnacles

Seashore shells

Most of the shells found on beaches are produced by a group of animals called molluscs. These vary in shape, but all have a head, a soft body and a muscular foot. There are over 800 species in Britain, mostly aquatic, with about 650 species living in the sea. When the animals die their shells are washed up on the shore.

Most molluscs have either single or double shells and are known as univalves or bivalves respectively. Univalve shells are usually spirally coiled and include winkles and needle shells. Bivalve shells may each be the same size (as in mussels), unequal (as in scallops) or very small in relation to the body (as in shipworms of the family *Teredinidae* whose small shells may be only one tenth the size of the animal itself. Many have a mother-of-pearl lining.

Common razor shell

Common mussel

Common mussels are found all around the coast below low tide mark where they are continually covered by water and can feed constantly. They form densely packed beds in areas sheltered from heavy seas. They usually grow to about 5cm long. They are hermaphrodites (i.e. have both male and female characteristics) and shed their eggs and sperm into the water in spring. Fertilised eggs develop into planktonic larvae which after several weeks of free life settle on shore to develop into adults. These have the familiar curved blue-black to dark brown shells, and live from 3-5 years.

Common razor shell

As the English name suggests, these shells are shaped like the blade of an old fashioned cut-throat razor. If found as living creatures on the foreshore they are capable of burrowing rapidly into the sand. The shells are a golden cream colour up to 15cm in length and often have a shiny 'varnished' look. They can be found singly, and sometimes joined. Breeding is in the summer, probably from about 3 years, with the life-span around 7-8 years. They are in decline in many areas due to overfishing.

Common limpets

Common limpet

Often abundant, firmly fixed to rocks and easily recognised by their thick, steeply conical shells up to 6 cm long. The outer shell surface has radiating ridges and well-marked growth lines, the inner surface being smooth greenish-grey. The mollusc clings to the rock with a sucker-like organ and may seek food up to a metre away when the tide is in, scraping algae off shore rocks, then returning at ebb tide. Limpets breed by shedding eggs into the sea between October and December. Their shells grow to fit a fixed spot on hard rock or the limpet grinds out a scar in soft rock. They may live to 15 years.

Flat periwinkle

The winkles are the most conspicuous and often the most abundant mesogastropods (animals with just a single kidney, gonad and gill, and varied reproductive stategies) living in the intertidal area, between the high and low waterlines. Winkles have spiral but rather globular shells; the shell opening or 'aperture' has a completely rounded lip.

Periwinkles

The Flat periwinkle varies its colour according to habitat: lighter shells occur on sheltered shores, and darker, chequered shells on exposed shores. Colours may range from creamy through to yellow and vivid orange. It is usually found on large brown seaweeds, such as Bladder wrack, on which it feeds and lays oval or kidney-shaped eggs in jelly-encased masses. Lives to 3 years or more.

Flat periwinkle feeding on seaweed

Thin tellins

Thin tellin
An irregularly oval shell which is thin, flat and brittle, as well as smooth and glossy with variable colour and banding. Grows to about 3cm long. Found in fine to medium sand areas and may be extremely abundant on suitable seashores. It is an important food for young plaice which crop the siphons of the tellins, although these quickly regenerate. Life expectancy is around 5 years.

Common cockle
The most familar edible cockle and often the most abundant. There are about 24 broad ribs crossed by concentric ridges which may have flat, short spines. Growth rings are distinct and the inner surfaces are dull and white. Found in all grades of sand.

Auger shell or Tower shell
Slender, flat-sided and sharply-pointed shell with around 20 whorls and a maximum length of 5.5 cm. Shells are often cast up on shore. The mollusc lives partly buried in silty sand or mud and its aperture appears squarish.

Common cockles

Auger shells are gregarious animals and very sedentary. Males shed sperm into water during reproduction, and this is simply filtered by the females. Every female produces several hundred round capsules at spawning: each capsule, holding up to 1000 eggs, is anchored to the female's shell or to shell fragments.

Common whelk
This is a large whelk up to 11cm in length, with a slightly stepped spiral ridge of 8 rounded whorls. There is a short open siphonal canal, never closed over, with the flexible siphon usually extending well beyond its edge. It feeds on cockles, other bivalves and carrion. Quite common, it is found on muddy sand and gravel and also on rock.

Needle whelk
A long thin spire with 12-15 whorls, and growing to 1cm long. Ribs and ridges form rows of tubercles, giving them a rather warty appearance. Aperture is flared, oval or angular. Found on muddy sand, often with *Zostera maritima* (also known as eel-grass or grass wrack) or among mud on sheltered rock.

Seahorse
The general form is well-known, with the head set at an angle to the body, the trunk short and portly looking, and the tail curled and tapering. The snout is straight. Brown, with small white spots and up to 15 cm long, the seahorse clings to seaweeds and grasses using its prehensile tail, or it swims upright. The male has a ventral brood pouch which is closed except for a small opening. It is particularly associated with south-west Britain and the Channel, and the National Marine Aquarium at Plymouth has a fine collection.

Starfish or Sand star
A rigid starfish found on fine to medium grade sand, usually partially buried. Feeding on bivalves, worms and crustaceans, it may grow to 20 cm in diameter. It has 5 arms or rays which regenerate if lost, so irregularly rayed specimens may occur.

Starfish together with a sea-horse

Common cuttlefish

A close relative of the squid, the cuttlefish is broadly oval and up to 40 cm long. Lateral fins run the entire length of the animal but are not joined at the rear, with the cuttlebone extending from behind the head to the posterior or rear end of the body. It is the cuttlebone that we find on the beach. All cuttlefish have four pairs of short and one pair of long tentacles, and each tentacle has four rows of suckers. Found on sandy and muddy substrata and offshore to 250 m. Moves inshore during summer months and spawns gregariously on shallow sandy bottoms.

Cuttlebone

The Beadlet is probably the most familiar inter-tidal sea anemone, common on rocky shores from the most exposed to the most sheltered

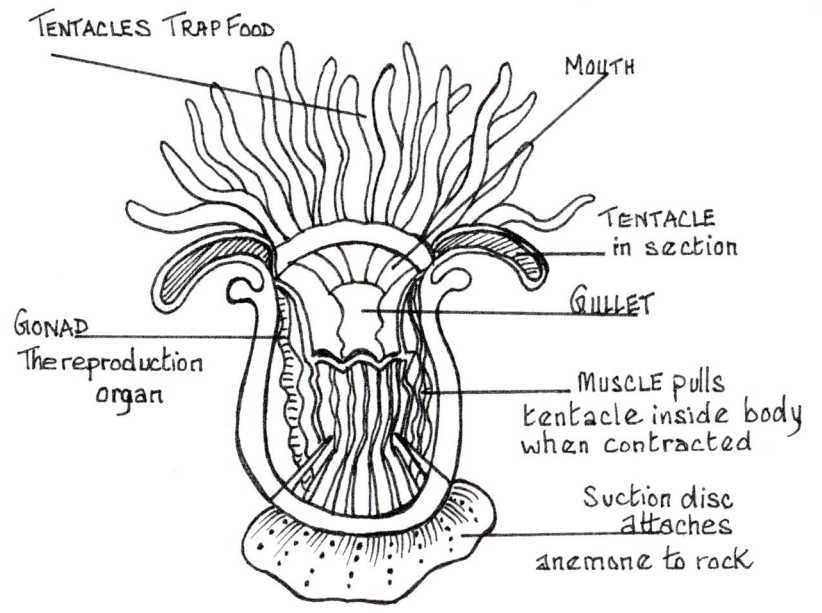

How a sea anemone feeds

Sea anemones

These flower-like animals are widespread around the Cornish coast. The numerous partitions in the anemone's stomach increase its digestive surface, allowing it to swallow and digest large animals such as fish and crabs. The Beadlet is probably the most familiar inter-tidal sea anemone. Fully expanded, the broad cyclindrical column may be 50 mm high.

Green shore crab
The most familiar crab, abundant on every type of seashore and well into estuaries and saltmarsh creeks. The carapace or shell has a maximum length of 6 cm and is somewhat wider than it is long. Rarely uniform green, usually patterned and very variable, especially juveniles. Intertidal including shore pools. Up to 185,000 eggs are laid, attached to the pleopods (limbs) of the female where they may remain for several months before hatching as planktonic larvae. Breeding follows the female's summer moult.

Ragworm
Used as bait by anglers; our picture shows ragworm tubes at the edge of the foreshore. The ragworm's body is flattened, with a prominent red blood vessel showing down the middle of the back. Of variable colour, it burrows into the mud, typically in sheltered areas or amongst eel grass, and may grow to 12 cm in length (the larger King Rag may grow to 25-40 cm). The big specimens can bite so beware!

Ragworm casts

Mermaid's purse

These are the egg cases of elasmobranch fish, which include the sharks and rays, and are quite commonly found along the strandline. When freshly laid they are olive brown and translucent, and the developing embryos can be clearly seen. Once cast up on the beach they dry out and darken as they harden, the oldest being quite black. Egg cases of skates and rays have a long curving spike at each corner, whilst those of dogfish have curling tendrils which help to secure them to seaweeds.

Mermaid's purse

Oystercatcher with young

Seashore birdlife
As you wander the seashore you may see gulls and other birds 'poking about', but their business on the beach is unlikely to be as aimless as yours. If you watch carefully you'll observe that with their differing bill lengths the birds are searching for food, probing at different levels in the sand and the mud, turning over stones or opening bivalves.

Bear in mind that birds and many other creatures may be nesting and raising young from April until well into the summer months, so please consider them. Very many bird species visit the shoreline (some of them illustrated in *Birds of Cornwall* in this series) but here are two species to look out for.

Oystercatcher
The Oystercatchers seen opposite with their two youngsters have nested on the cliffs nearby and have brought the chicks down to the tideline to find what food may be available. They feed principally on molluscs, cockles, mussels and limpets, with the occasional worm and a few insects also taken.

Ringed plover
The Ringed plover lays its eggs on shingle areas of the seashore and these are so well camouflaged as to be almost invisible to predators and ourselves. They are extremely vulnerable to tramping feet on the seashore, so pay close attention to where you are walking on the beach between March and August when the plovers may be trying to raise two or three broods. In an attempt to lure people away, these birds often feign injury.

Ringed plover's nest

Common seal

Common seal and Grey or Atlantic seal
The Common seal is the smaller of the two species that breed in Britain and is actually less common than the Grey seal. They may be seen in estuarine habitats and areas of seashore close to river mouths merging with the sea where they often haul themselves out of the water to bask.

It is not easy to tell these species apart by their colouring. The Common seal has a mottle of dark spots on a steely grey-black ground, but this is variable, and the Grey seal is so variable that its colour is all but useless for identification.

Grey or Atlantic seal

   The two species do, however, vary in head shape: the Common seal has a snub-nosed face, whereas the Grey or Atlantic seal has a longer, straight nose. The pictures show head-shapes of the Common and Grey seals.

   Both species have a gestation period of about 9 months and one young or 'pup' is born (June/July for Common seal and September–December, very occasionally spring, for Grey seal). Lifespan for males is 20 years for the Common seal and 25 for the Grey seal. Females live 15–20 years longer. Food is mainly fish, with shellfish and some invertebrates taken.

Above: dog prints
Below: otter prints

Tracks and signs

Seashore sand and mud often hold the imprints of birds and other animals – it's sometimes possible to work out which creatures have been out and about.

Dog prints

The commonest footprints, apart from our own, are dog prints, usually clearly showing four toes and claws. Fox prints are similar but narrower, and show as a straight and narrow set of tracks. When trotting, the fox sets a purposeful course whereas a dog tends to be more erratic, with frequent pauses and side-tracking as it sniffs around.

Otter prints

An exciting find, the tracks of an adult otter are the size of those of a medium-sized dog but contain five toes, not four. Again the animal's claws usually show clearly in the footprints. Otters are making a stong come-back in the West Country after a century of decline.

Gull prints

Bird prints

Birds' footprints may be numerous and often impossible to identify, though herons, moorhens and herring gulls leave well-indented and distinctive prints. It can be interesting to watch a bird moving about on sand or mud and then to see just what shaped prints it has left. The photograph shows the prints of a herring gull.

Bladder wrack in a tidal pool

Seaweed

All seaweeds are algae. They are found around the coasts in sheltered and rocky areas to a depth of a hundred metres in clear water, requiring light for their growth.

They are divided into four main groups based on their colours: blue-green, green, brown and red, although the division may not always be obvious.

Wracks are members of the brown group, with Bladder wrack easily identified by its paired, almost spherical, gas-filled 'bladders', which also give it the name popweed. Dark olive-brown and growing to 1 m long, its reproductive bodies form swollen forked tips to their branches.

The photograph on the page opposite shows the form *Fucus ceranoides* which has bladders and prefers sheltered areas.

Spiral or Flat wrack has a prominent midrib and no gas bladders. The fronds tend to twist spirally, though this is not a reliable character for identification. Reproductive bodies form rounded swollen tips to their branches, usually in pairs with each having a narrow rim as a continuation of the flat frond around its 'equator'. Olive brown. 150-200 mm long. Sheltered shores.

Spiral or Flat wrack

Mermaid's tresses
A narrow gas-filled cord growing up to 6 metres long with a minute holdfast (the part by which it fixes itself to a rock). It grows on gravel in shallow water, often in dense patches, and will tolerate brackish conditions.